C61 0365048 9E

D1635425

The Oxford Nursery Treasury

For Lily

The
Oxford Nursery
Treasury

Ian Beck

OXFORD
UNIVERSITY PRESS

Contents

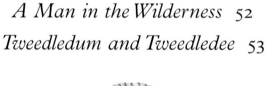

BELFAST PUBLIC LIBRARIES
SCHOOLS

The Princess and the Pea

Once upon a time, in a faraway kingdom, there lived a prince. He was an only child, and spoilt a little by his parents. For his twentieth birthday he was given a fine white stallion, called Blaze. One day his father sent for the prince. 'My boy,' he said, 'it is time you set out and found yourself a real princess to marry.' So the prince travelled the length and breadth of the world on Blaze. They rode through summer sun and winter snow. They rode under all the phases of the moon, through deserts and over mountains.

The prince met many girls who said that they were princesses. Girls who curtsied very nicely. Girls with eyes hidden behind painted fans. Girls who danced elegantly in bright, silk dresses. But the prince was never sure if any of them was a real princess. The king and queen had insisted, 'She must be a real princess.' But after all his travels, the prince had never been sure whether any of the girls he had met had been a real princess.

And so, one night, under a new moon, the prince rode back into the palace yard, with his head bowed and a heavy heart. His mother welcomed him back with his favourite meal. 'Come on,' she said, 'sausages, onion gravy, and mashed potatoes. I cooked them myself, this ought to cheer you up.'

But although the prince made a hearty supper, he was still sad. 'I've looked over the whole world, from one end to the other. I'll never find a real princess,' and he sighed.

'Don't worry,' said the queen, 'there are ways of telling a real princess. When the right girl comes, I will find out for you, never fear.'

Summer turned to autumn, and great storms shook the kingdom. Hailstones the size of goose eggs crashed around the palace turrets. A great wind tore up the ancient oak that the prince had played in since his childhood. Then winter came, howling in on a blizzard, and the palace was surrounded with deep drifts of snow; even Blaze was kept in the stable under fleecy blankets.

Then one night, the coldest of the year so far, when even the powdered snow had frozen into hard ice, there was a knocking at the palace door. The king was roused from his warm fireside. 'Who on earth can that be out in this awful weather, and at this late hour?' He set off, wrapped in his warmest cloak, and opened the heavy door.

A girl stood knee deep in a drift of snow. Her fine cape, reduced to rags, was wrapped around her shoulders, and she was huddled and shivering. Her hair was wet around her face, and there were little icicles on her sooty eyelashes. She fell into the king's arms, and he carried her into the warm parlour.

After a few minutes the girl was warmed through. She sat by the fire, drinking a cup of hot chocolate. Some colour had come back into her cheeks, and as she brushed the strands of damp hair away from her face, the prince could see that she might just be beautiful.

The queen stole a glance at her son, and noticed that he was a little smitten with the mysterious girl. 'Tell us about yourself, my dear,' said the queen.

'I am Princess Phoebe,' said the girl. 'I have been travelling the world, seeking a suitable prince to marry.' She shook her head sadly. 'I had searched for nearly a year with no luck, for you see he must be a real prince. I was just on my way home when the blizzard struck. I stabled my poor horse, and then followed the lights here.'

The prince was about to speak out when the queen gestured to him to be quiet. Then she said brightly, 'Well, my dear, you must be exhausted. You must have a hot bath, then we will put you to bed, and in the morning all shall be well.'

While Phoebe was in her bath, the queen took the prince and two servants to the guest bedchamber. She ordered the servants to strip all the bedding from the bed, and start over again. When the mattress was removed the queen took a little silver box from her purse, opened the box, and inside was a single green pea.

The queen took the pea and placed it in the middle of the bed base. Then she ordered the servants to bring as many mattresses and feather quilts as could be found. She had all the mattresses piled one on top of the other, along with all the quilts and covers. When they had finished there must have been fifty or more, reaching almost to the ceiling, and it was a very tall room.

'Now we shall see if she is a real princess,' said the queen. 'Trust me.'

Princess Phoebe spent an uncomfortable night. Despite the duvets, feather mattresses, and cosy warmth, things weren't right. No matter how she lay in the bed, no matter how she twisted and turned, this way and that, it was no good, she couldn't settle, and through all that night she didn't sleep a wink.

In the morning, all looked beautiful in the bright sunshine. This would be a fine place to live, Phoebe thought, looking across the snow-covered kingdom from the high window. She went down to the parlour for breakfast.

'Good morning, my dear,' said the queen. 'I hope you slept well.'

Phoebe looked tired, and her eyes had dark circles round them. 'I have never spent a more uncomfortable night,' she said. 'I couldn't sleep at all. No matter how I lay in the bed it felt as if something was digging into me.

I must be covered in bruises.'

It was then that the prince understood what his mother had been doing. If this girl had felt such a tiny thing as a pea through all those layers of quilts and feathers, then she must be a real princess.

'Look around you, my dear,' said the queen. 'You will see that this is no ordinary house, it is a palace.'

Phoebe looked at all the silverware on the breakfast table; the fine damasks and silks at the tall windows. At that moment the king entered, dressed in his state robes and accompanied by his lord chamberlain, who carried a crown on a velvet cushion.

'If this is a palace,' said Phoebe, 'then you must be the queen, and there, if I am not mistaken, is the king.' At that she curtsied, and then bounced up with a smile on her face. 'Which means that your son is a real prince.'

Later that day the princess's horse was brought from the stables, a fine black mare with a long silky tail. Together the prince and princess set off to ride in the bright winter sunshine. There was even a promise of spring in the air. 'Mark my words,' said the queen, 'we'd best set the lord chamberlain to preparing the cathedral for a royal wedding.'

And so they did, and later that year the real prince and the real princess were married, and went to live in their own palace by a lake with a good stable for both their fine horses. Soon they had to add a nursery, and so they all lived happily to the end of their days, which was as long a time as it could be.

Jack a Nory

I'll tell you a story
About Jack a Nory,
And now my story's begun;
I'll tell you another
Of Jack and his brother,
And now my story is done.

Ride a Cock-Horse

Ride a cock-horse to Banbury Cross,
To see a fine lady upon a white horse;
Rings on her fingers and bells on her toes,
And she shall have music wherever she goes.

Pease Porridge Hot

Pease porridge hot,
Pease porridge cold,
Pease porridge in the pot
Nine days old.
Some like it hot,
Some like it cold,
Some like it in the pot
Nine days old.

Apple Pie

Apple-pie, apple-pie,
Peter likes apple-pie;
So do I, so do I.

Roses are Red

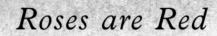

Roses are red,
   Violets are blue,
Sugar is sweet
   And so are you.

Lilies are White

Lilies are white,
Rosemary's green,
When I am king,
You shall be queen.

The Tortoise and
the Hare

Once upon a time, and as long ago as anyone can remember, there lived a tortoise. His was a slow, steady, and pleasant life. Every winter, while the world was cold and harsh, he would fill up on sweet lettuce and carrots, and then fall fast asleep in his cosy home, until the spring.

Just near the tortoise lived an excitable and bouncy hare. He rushed everywhere at great speed, especially in the spring, when he seemed to be full of extra energy.

So it was one spring morning, when the hare rushed past his neighbour the tortoise on the road. The tortoise had been ambling along, minding his own business. He had only just woken up from his long winter sleep, and was just getting used to the world again, when he was nearly knocked over by the dashing hare.

'Hey, watch where you are going,' said the tortoise. 'We can't all rush about like you.'

'My word,' said the hare, 'but you are a slowcoach.'

Now the tortoise was cross at having been nearly knocked over, and he answered quite snappily, 'Not as slow as you seem to think. Why, I could beat you in a race any day.'

'Oh, really,' said the hare with a laugh. 'I wouldn't bet on it if I were you.'

Just then a fox strolled past, and the hare said, 'This tortoise says he can beat me in a race,' and they both laughed, so that the tortoise got even crosser.

He said, 'I bet you my snug winter den that I can beat you over any distance.'

'I'll bet you a lifetime supply of sweet lettuce and carrots that you can't,' said the hare.

Then the fox said, 'You shall run a race, and I shall judge the winner.'

'Agreed,' said the tortoise and the hare together, and the hare added, 'Easiest bet I've ever won,' and laughed again. The tortoise said nothing, just smiled and shook his head.

So it was that the fox set up a course across the countryside with a start and finish line, and on a bright morning the tortoise and the hare lined up ready to start.

The fox raised his flag, and said, 'Ready,' and the hare raised himself up on his strong back legs, while the tortoise just stood and waited. Then the fox said, 'Steady,' and the hare breathed heavily and puffed out his cheeks, running on the spot, while the tortoise just stood and waited. Then the fox said 'Go!' and dropped the flag, and the hare sprinted away as fast as he could, while the tortoise just ambled forward in a slow and steady way.

The hare ran fast for a while. Then he slowed a little and looked back down the road. There was no sign of the tortoise, he had been left far behind. The hare laughed to himself and stopped altogether. It was a warm morning, and running so fast was tiring work. The hare spotted a nice patch of shade under a tree, and he went and sat there to wait for the tortoise.

'It'll be a long wait,' he said, and yawned and stretched. 'I'll just have a little nap.' So the hare settled under the tree and soon fell fast asleep.

The tortoise meanwhile was walking along, not fast, but sure and steady. As it was so warm, and he was hot inside his shell, he stopped and had a nibble of some cooling dandelion leaves, and a drink from a stream. The sun rose higher and hotter, and he ambled on, slow but sure. After what seemed a very long time he drew level with, and then just overtook, a snail. 'Morning, Mr Snail,' said the tortoise.

'Morning, Mr Tortoise,' said the snail. 'If you look over there you can see the hare asleep under that tree.'

'Why, so he is,' said the tortoise, and he shook his head and carried on, and on, down the dusty road.

The hare woke from his refreshing nap. He felt fine, if a little stiff. He stretched and ran up and down for a bit, to ease himself in for the run. Then he climbed the tree and looked back down the road. There was no sign of the tortoise but he could just see a snail, far away on the road. He turned round and he could see the road going the other way, and far off he could see the finish line with the bright banner, and a crowd of animals waiting. He was about to jump down and do some push-ups before setting off again, when he saw something on the road that caused him to fall down from the tree in shock. It was the tortoise plodding along, only yards from the finish line.

The hare picked himself up, and set off again as fast as he could. He crested the hill at great speed, and there, some way ahead of him, was the tortoise, making steady progress, and now only a few feet from the finish line. The hare made a great effort and charged down the final straight. He crossed the line and fell out of breath to the ground. He was too late. The tortoise had crossed the line long before the hare, and was being congratulated by the fox.

'That's a lifetime of sweet lettuce and carrots that the hare owes me,' said the tortoise, with a big smile. 'You see, hare, slow and steady does it.'

And the tortoise lived for a very, very, very long time (as tortoises do) and for all of that time the hare had to make sure he had lots and lots of sweet lettuce and carrots. Except during the long cold winter, of course, when the tortoise was snug and asleep in his burrow, and the hare had all that long, cold time to himself.

Dickery, Dickery, Dare

Dickery, dickery, dare,
The pig flew up in the air;
The man in brown
Soon brought him down,
Dickery, dickery, dare.

See-Saw, Margery Daw

See-saw, Margery Daw,
Jacky shall have a new master;
Jacky shall have but a penny a day,
Because he can't work any faster.

See-saw, Margery Daw,
The old hen flew over the malt house;
She counted her chickens one by one,
Still she missed the little white one,
And this is it, this is it, this is it.

Little Poll Parrot

Little Poll Parrot
Sat in his garret
Eating toast and tea;
A little brown mouse
Jumped into the house,
And stole it all away.

Hoddley, Poddley

Hoddley, poddley, puddle and fogs,
Cats are to marry the poodle dogs;
Cats in blue jackets and dogs in red hats,
What will become of the mice and the rats?

Sing a Song of Sixpence

Sing a song of sixpence,
    A pocket full of rye;
Four and twenty blackbirds,
    Baked in a pie.

When the pie was opened,
    The birds began to sing;
Was not that a dainty dish,
    To set before the king?

The king was in his counting-house,
　　Counting out his money;
The queen was in the parlour,
　　Eating bread and honey.

The maid was in the garden,
　　Hanging out the clothes,
When down came a blackbird
　　And pecked off her nose.

Diddlety, Diddlety, Dumpty

Diddlety, diddlety, dumpty,
The cat ran up the plum tree;
Half a crown to fetch her down,
Diddlety, diddlety, dumpty.

There Was an Old Crow

There was an old crow
   Sat upon a clod;
That's the end of my song.
   —That's odd.

The Porridge Pot

Once upon a time, when the world was a place of forests and magic, there lived a little girl called Ragamuffin. She lived with her mother, in a tiny wooden house, in a tiny village on the edge of a great dark forest. Her mother was very poor, and did the best she could to feed and clothe herself and her little daughter.

However, as autumn ended, and the cold and darkness of winter approached, things went from bad to worse. At last the larder was bare, and there was nothing left for them to eat.

'Don't worry, mother,' said kind little Ragamuffin. 'There may be a few berries left in among the trees. I'll see if I can find some.' And so Ragamuffin set out with her basket on her arm. She walked among the tall trees. It was damp and misty, and gradually Ragamuffin found herself walking deeper and deeper along the twisty paths. She found no berries, no mushrooms, no nuts, nothing.

It was a cold morning, and she shivered and drew her thin cloak around her little shoulders. It was just then that she heard something. A twig cracked and some leaves rustled under the trees. Ragamuffin was frightened. She had heard of the fierce wolves that sometimes prowled about in the deep forest.

But then she heard a friendly voice. 'Is that you, my little Ragamuffin?' And an old lady appeared, leaning on a stout walking stick. She stepped forward from the mist under the trees. 'I know you, little Ragamuffin,' she said.

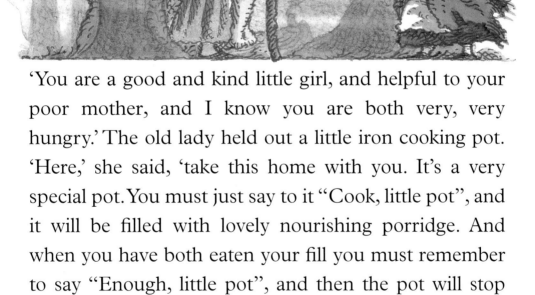

'You are a good and kind little girl, and helpful to your poor mother, and I know you are both very, very hungry.' The old lady held out a little iron cooking pot. 'Here,' she said, 'take this home with you. It's a very special pot. You must just say to it "Cook, little pot", and it will be filled with lovely nourishing porridge. And when you have both eaten your fill you must remember to say "Enough, little pot", and then the pot will stop making the porridge.'

Ragamuffin took the pot and thanked the old lady. Then she ran back home to her mother as fast as she could, clutching the little pot under her cloak.

When she arrived back at the little house, her mother was sitting at the table, her head sunk in despair. Ragamuffin set the little pot on the bare wooden table. 'Cook, little pot,' she said. At once the kitchen filled with the smell of fresh, warm porridge. Her mother looked up. There was a friendly bubbly sound, and the little pot filled to the brim with what looked like steaming porridge. It was the most delicious porridge they had ever tasted, just sweet enough, and tasting as though it were made with cream fresh from the cow. They ate and ate until they could eat no more. Ragamuffin said, 'Enough, little pot,' and the pot was empty again.

For most of that long, cold winter, Ragamuffin and her mother ate together from the little pot. The porridge stayed as fresh and delicious as ever. Then, one day, Ragamuffin's mother was alone in the house. She thought it could do no harm to have some of the delicious porridge on her own. She fetched the little pot down from its special shelf, and set it down on the table.

She waited for a moment in anticipation, and then said, 'Cook, little pot.' There came the familiar delicious smell, then the little bubbly noise, and then the pot was full, and the mother ate her fill, and then a little more, and then even some more, so that her tummy was nicely warm and rounded. Then the mother closed her eyes in contentment, and fell fast asleep.

She woke up a little later, with the feeling that her chair was afloat on a warm sea. She opened her eyes, and let out a cry. 'OH NO!' The little pot was still bubbling over with porridge. The porridge was pouring over the edge of the pot, it was running all over the table, down the legs, and had filled all the floor of the little house up to the window.

Her chair was floating on a sea of porridge. She held on to the edge of the table and called out to Ragamuffin. You see, she had forgotten the words that would stop the little pot.

She did her best. She called out, 'Do stop all this,' and 'No more porridge,' and, 'That's enough,' but it was no good. More and more porridge kept bubbling out of the pot. It poured through the windows and under the door, it swept through the streets of the little village like a great wave. It swept up under the doors and through the windows of the other villagers, and gradually all the village houses filled up with porridge. One by one the people struggled out through their front doors or windows. Their clothes were covered in the sticky porridge, but goodness it did taste delicious.

At that moment Ragamuffin came home. She shook her head as she stepped through the river of porridge; she had to try hard to keep from bursting out laughing. Just then her greedy mother came floating out of the window on her chair. 'Oh, help, Ragamuffin,' she called out. Then Ragamuffin and all the villagers laughed, and Ragamuffin said, 'Enough, little pot,' and the flow of porridge stopped, and her mother's chair came to a slow and sticky halt.

It took the village the rest of the winter to eat their way through all the lovely porridge. But at least nobody went hungry that year.

A Man in the Wilderness

A man in the wilderness asked me,
How many strawberries grow in the sea.
I answered him, as I thought good,
As many red herrings as swim in the wood.

Tweedledum and Tweedledee

Tweedledum and Tweedledee
   Agreed to have a battle,
For Tweedledum said Tweedledee
   Had spoiled his nice new rattle.
Just then flew by a monstrous crow
   As big as a tar-barrel,
Which frightened both the heroes so,
   They quite forgot their quarrel.

If All the World Was Paper

If all the world was paper,
   And all the sea was ink,
If all the trees were bread and cheese,
   What should we have to drink?

Pretty Maid, Pretty Maid

Pretty maid, pretty maid,
   Where have you been?
Gathering roses
   To give to the queen.
Pretty maid, pretty maid,
   What gave she you?
She gave me a diamond,
   As big as my shoe.

Mr Punchinello

Oh, mother, I shall be married to Mr Punchinello,
    To Mr Punch,
    To Mr Joe,
    To Mr Nell,
    To Mr Lo,
    Mr Punch, Mr Joe,
    Mr Nell, Mr Lo,
    To Mr Punchinello.

Sally Go Round the Sun

Sally go round the sun,
Sally go round the moon,
Sally go round the chimney-pots
On a Saturday afternoon.

Chicken Licken

Once upon a time, when the world was young and the animals could speak, there was a tiny wee chick called Chicken Licken. Now it happened that fluffy, yellow Chicken Licken was grubbing about in her favourite patch, when an acorn fell, 'plomp', on her little tail. 'Oh no,' said Chicken Licken, 'the sky is falling down. Help, I must go and warn the king.'

So she set off on her busy little feet, and after a while she met her great friend Henny Penny.

'Well well, if it isn't Chicken Licken,' said Henny Penny. 'Where are you off to in such a hurry?'

'Quick, help help, Henny Penny. The sky is falling down, and I must go and warn the king.'

'I see,' said Henny Penny. 'And how can you be so sure that the sky is falling down?'

'Because,' said Chicken Licken, 'I saw it with my own two eyes, heard it with my own two ears, and a piece of the sky landed, plomp, on my own tail.'

'Then I'll come with you,' said Henny Penny.

So they set off together, and tripped along through the grass, until they met Cocky Locky.

'Well, a-doodle well,' said Cocky Locky to Henny Penny and Chicken Licken. 'Where are you two going, may I ask a-doodle do?'

'Oh, help, Cocky Locky. The sky is falling down, and we must go and warn the king.'

'I see,' said Cocky Locky. 'And how do you know the sky is falling a-doodle down?'

'Chicken Licken told me,' said Henny Penny.

'I saw it with my own two eyes, heard it with my own two ears, and a piece of the sky landed, plomp, on my tail,' said Chicken Licken.

'Very well,' said Cocky Locky, 'I will travel with you, and we will warn the king.'

So all three set off skipping through the grass, until they met Ducky Daddles.

'Well, well, well, quack, well,' said Ducky Daddles. 'If it isn't Cocky Locky, Henny Penny, and Chicken Licken. Where are you all off to?'

'Oh, help a-doodle do, the sky is falling down, and we must go and warn the king.'

'But how do you know the sky is falling down?' asked Ducky Daddles.

'Well, Henny Penny told me,' said Cocky Locky.

'Yes, and Chicken Licken told me,' said Henny Penny.

'I saw it with my own two eyes, heard it with my own two ears, and a piece of it landed, plomp, on my own tail,' said Chicken Licken.

'Then I had better, quack, come with you, and we can all warn the king.'

So they set off together, on their brisk little feet, until they met Goosey Loosey.

'A very good morning to you, Ducky Daddles, Cocky Locky, Henny Penny, and Chicken Licken. Where might you all be going in such a rush?'

'Oh, help, Goosey Loosey, the sky is falling down and we must go and warn the king.'

'But how do you know that the sky is falling down?' asked Goosey Loosey, looking up at the bright blue above.

'Cocky Locky told me,' said Ducky Daddles.

'Henny Penny told me,' said Cocky Locky.

'Chicken Licken told me,' said Henny Penny.

'I saw it with my own two eyes, I heard it with my own two ears, and a piece of it landed, plomp, on my own tail,' said Chicken Licken.

'I think I had better come with you, and together we can all warn the king,' said Goosey Loosey.

So they all set off in a busy little line, until they met Turkey Lurkey.

'Goodness gracious me,' said Turkey Lurkey. 'Goosey Loosey, Ducky Daddles, Cocky Locky, Henny Penny, and Chicken Licken! What a fine feathered sight on such a morning. Where are you all trotting off to?'

'Oh, you must help us, Turkey Lurkey. The sky is falling down, and we must go and warn the king.'

'But how do you know the sky is falling down?' said Turkey Lurkey.

'Ducky Daddles told me,' said Goosey Loosey.

'Cocky Locky told me,' said Ducky Daddles.

'Henny Penny told me,' said Cocky Locky.

'Chicken Licken told me,' said Henny Penny.

'I saw it with my own two eyes, and heard it with my own two ears, and a piece of it landed, plomp, on my own tail,' said Chicken Licken.

'I think I had better come with you. Yes, that's the best thing, then we can all warn the king together,' said Turkey Lurkey.

So off they all went, smallest in front, biggest at the back, until they met Mr Foxy Woxy.

'Mmmm, good morning,' said Mr Foxy Woxy. 'Well, well, if it isn't Turkey Lurkey, Goosey Loosey, Ducky Daddles, Cocky Locky, Henny Penny, and Chicken Licken. Where are you all going to on such a fine morning?'

'Oh, help, Mr Foxy Woxy. The sky is falling down, and we must go and warn the king!'

'But how do you know the sky is falling down?' asked Mr Foxy Woxy.

'Goosey Loosey told me,' said Turkey Lurkey.

'Ducky Daddles told me,' said Goosey Loosey.

'Cocky Locky told me,' said Ducky Daddles.

'Henny Penny told me,' said Cocky Locky.

'Chicken Licken told me,' said Henny Penny.

'I saw it with my own two eyes, and heard it with my own two ears, and a piece of it landed, plomp, on my own tail,' said Chicken Licken.

'Then we shall all run together as fast as we can to my little den, for safety, and then I will warn the king,' said Mr Foxy Woxy.

So all together they scurried on their busy little feet into the dark den of Mr Foxy Woxy. And so it was that the king was never warned that the sky was falling down.

Sing, Sing

Sing, sing,
    What shall I sing?
The cat's run away
    With the pudding string!
Do, do,
    What shall I do?
The cat's run away
    With the pudding too!

Dance to Your Daddy

Dance to your daddy,
　My little babby,
Dance to your daddy,
　My little lamb.

You shall have a fishy
　In a little dishy,
You shall have a fishy
　When the boat comes in.

You shall have an apple,
　You shall have a plum,
You shall have a rattle-basket
　When your daddy comes home.

69

Bobby Shaftoe

Bobby Shaftoe's gone to sea,
Silver buckles at his knee;
He'll come back and marry me,
Bonny Bobby Shaftoe.

Dame Trot

Dame Trot and her cat
   Sat down for a chat;
The Dame sat on this side
   And puss sat on that.

Puss, says the Dame,
   Can you catch a rat,
Or a mouse in the dark?
   Purr, says the cat.

The Brave Old Duke of York

Oh, the brave old Duke of York,
He had ten thousand men;
He marched them up to the top of the hill,
And then he marched them down again.
And when they were up, they were up,
And when they were down, they were down,
And when they were only halfway up,
They were neither up nor down.

Clap Hands

Clap hands, Daddy comes
With his pocket full of plums,
And a cake for Johnny.

The Old Woman in a Shoe

There was an old woman who lived in a shoe,
She had so many children she didn't know what to do;
She gave them some broth without any bread;
She whipped them all soundly and put them to bed.

Lazy Jack

Once upon a time, a long time ago, when the world was still full of marvels, there was a boy called Jack. He lived with his mother at the edge of a fine country town. They were very poor, and Jack's mother did as best she could, and worked very hard for their living. She knitted woollen socks for all the local gentry. She worked from dawn till dusk, wearing out her poor old fingers. Her son Jack, on the other hand, did nothing. During the hot summer months he would sit around in the garden, fanning himself.

Then he would hog the best of the fireplace during the long cold winters.

Everyone shook their heads and called him Lazy Jack. His mother did her best, but she could never persuade him to lift a finger to help. Finally, one day she said that, 'enough was enough'. He must go out and work to help pay his way, or she would turn him into the street, and no one would want to help Lazy Jack!

Now this worried Jack, and bright and early the next morning he set off for a nearby farm. There he was hired to help, and at the end of the day he was paid with a shiny new penny. Jack walked home slowly in the evening sun. He spun his penny up in the air and generally showed it off to everyone, for he had never earned a whole penny before.

When he was nearly home, Jack lost the penny. It dropped in the water as he crossed the stream. His mother shook her head. 'I knew you were lazy, Jack, now it turns out you're daft as well. You should have put that penny safely in your pocket.'

'I will remember next time,' sighed Jack.

So early the next morning Jack set out and was given a job helping with the cows. At the end of the day, Jack was paid with a handsome jug of creamy fresh milk. Jack remembered what had happened to his penny. So he put the jug of milk deep into his trouser pocket, and set off home. By the time he got there, he had spilled all the milk, and the jug was empty.

'Oh dear me, Jack,' said his mother, 'what will become of you? You should have carried that on your silly head.'

'I will remember next time,' said Jack.

The next morning Jack set off in good heart to another farm. He was given a day's work helping in the dairy. At the end of the day, Jack was paid with a great round of delicious cream cheese.

'Mother will be pleased,' thought Jack, and, remembering what had happened to the milk in his pocket, he popped the round of soft cheese on top of his head and set off in the warm evening sun to walk home.

By the time he got home the cheese had melted and spoiled. It had run into his hair, and all down his shirt in a great sticky mess.

'I don't know, Jack,' said his mother. 'What a waste. Your shirt's ruined, and as for your hair, I can't even look. You should have carried that fine cheese carefully in your hands.'

'Sorry, mother,' said Jack. 'I will remember next time.'

The next morning Jack set out at cock-crow and was given a day's work by the baker. Jack worked hard all day in the hot bakery, and the baker paid him with a fine ginger tom-cat. Now Jack remembered what had happened to the cream cheese, so he took the tom-cat and began to carry it home very carefully in his hands. But this was a fierce and proud cat, and it began to yowl, and wriggle, and scratch. So much so that Jack had to let it go.

When he got home his mother could scarcely believe it. 'My word Jack, but you are a nincompoop. You should have tied a string around the cat and pulled 'im along behind you.'

'Sorry, mother,' said Jack. 'I will remember next time.'

Early the following morning, Jack found work from the butcher, and at the end of the day the butcher paid Jack with a fine ham on the bone. Now his mother would be pleased, it was just the thing to serve with a boiled cabbage. Then Jack remembered what had happened to the cat, so he tied a piece of string to the ham and pulled it all the way home behind him, through all the mud, and mess, and muddle of the streets. By the time he got home, of course, there was barely a shank of bone left at the end of the string: the ham was ruined.

His mother finally lost her temper, and fetched him a clout on the head. 'You're as daft as a brush. Now we've just cabbage for our dinner. You should have carried it on your shoulder.'

'Ow,' said Jack. 'Sorry, mother. I will remember next time.'

The next day Jack was hired by a wealthy merchant, who lived in a fine house nearby. Now this merchant was a widower who had a beautiful daughter. The daughter was very sad; she had neither laughed nor spoken for many years. All that week she had seen Jack from her window as he went off to his various jobs. Every evening she had watched him come home again.

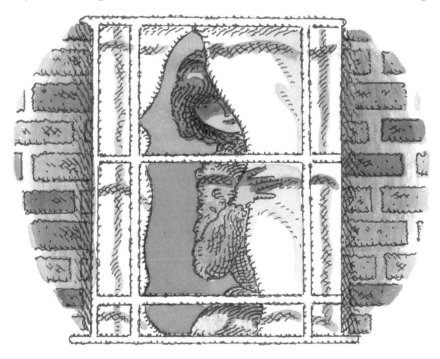

She had seen him lose his penny in the stream. She had seen him with milk spilling from his pocket. She had seen him with a great cream cheese melting into his hair. She had seen him struggling with a fierce tom-cat. She had seen him pulling a ham through the streets on a piece of string. Each time she had felt a little cheered up by the sight of Lazy Jack. (He was, after all, not a bad looking lad.) She could feel herself thawing inside like the river at the end of a long winter.

At the end of the day, the merchant rewarded Jack with a fine young donkey. Now Jack remembered what had happened to the ham, and with a great effort he swung the donkey up on to his shoulders. He began to stagger home with it. The merchant's daughter saw Jack from her window. He looked so silly trudging along with the donkey upside down across his shoulders and with its legs sticking up above his head, that she burst into great peals of golden laughter.

The merchant was so delighted to have his daughter restored to her old self that he sent for Jack and rewarded him with a gold sovereign. Jack straightaway put the sovereign in his pocket to keep it safe. Later in the year Jack married the merchant's beautiful daughter, and his mother was able to retire from knitting socks. She lived with them in their fine house, for the rest of her days, which was a very long time indeed.

Teddy Bear, Teddy Bear

Teddy bear, teddy bear, touch the ground,
Teddy bear, teddy bear, turn right round,
Teddy bear, teddy bear, go upstairs,
Teddy bear, teddy bear, say your prayers,
Teddy bear, teddy bear, switch off the light,
Teddy bear, teddy bear, say Goodnight.

Rock-a-Bye, Baby

Rock-a-bye, baby,
   Thy cradle is green,
Father's a nobleman,
   Mother's a queen;
And Betty's a lady,
   And wears a gold ring;
And Johnny's a drummer,
   And drums for the king.

There Was an Old Woman

There was an old woman tossed up in a basket,
   Seventeen times as high as the moon;
Where she was going I couldn't but ask it,
   For in her hand she carried a broom.
   Old woman, old woman, old woman, quoth I,
   Where are you going to up so high?
   To brush the cobwebs off the sky!
   May I go with you? Aye, by-and-by.

Blow, Wind, Blow

Blow, wind, blow!
  And go, mill, go!
That the miller may grind his corn;
  That the baker may take it,
  And into bread make it,
And bring us a loaf in the morn.

Down with the Lambs

Down with the lambs,
   Up with the lark,
Run to bed, children
   Before it gets dark.

BELFAST PUBLIC LIBRARIES

SCHOOLS

Go to Bed, Tom

Go to bed, Tom,
Go to bed, Tom,
Tired or not, Tom,
Go to bed, Tom.

Index of Titles and First Lines of Poems

OXFORD
UNIVERSITY PRESS

Great Clarendon Street, Oxford OX2 6DP

Oxford University Press is a department of the University of Oxford.
It furthers the University's objective of excellence in research, scholarship,
and education by publishing worldwide in

Oxford New York

Auckland Bangkok Buenos Aires
Cape Town Chennai Dar es Salaam Delhi Hong Kong Istanbul
Karachi Kolkata Kuala Lumpur Madrid Melbourne Mexico City Mumbai
Nairobi São Paulo Shanghai Singapore Taipei Tokyo Toronto

With an associated company in Berlin

Oxford is a registered trade mark of Oxford University Press
in the UK and in certain other countries

Text and illustrations copyright © Ian Beck 2000

The moral rights of the author/artist have been asserted

First published 2000
First published in paperback 2002

All rights reserved. No part of this publication may be reproduced,
stored in a retrieval system, or transmitted, in any form or by any means,
without the prior permission in writing of Oxford University Press.
Within the UK, exceptions are allowed in respect of any fair dealing for the
purpose of research or private study, or criticism or review, as permitted
under the Copyright, Designs and Patents Act 1988, or in the case of
reprographic reproductioh in accordance with the terms of the licences
issued by the Copyright Licensing Agency. Enquiries concerning
reproduction outside these terms and in other countries should be
sent to the Rights Department, Oxford University Press,
at the above address.

This book is sold subject to the condition that it shall not, by way
of trade or otherwise, be lent, re-sold, hired out or otherwise circulated
without the publisher's prior consent in any form of binding or cover
other than that in which it is published and without a similar condition
including this condition being imposed on the subsequent purchaser.

British Library Cataloguing in Publication Data available

ISBN 0 19 278164 2 (hardback)
ISBN 0 19 278193 6 (paperback)

Typeset by Mary Tudge Typesetting Services

Printed in Spain by Graficas Estella